ACING YOUR MARRIAGE-BASED GREEN CARD INTERVIEW

by Attorney Ekaterina B. Huff

Jacobs & Whitehall
21750 Hardy Oak Blvd
Suite 104 – 51700
San Antonio, Texas 78258
www.jacobsandwhitehall.com

Ordering Information:

Quantity sales. Special discounts are available on quantity purchases by corporations, associations, and others. For details, contact the publisher at the address above.

Orders by U.S. trade bookstores and wholesalers. Please contact Jacobs & Whitehall: Tel: (888) 991-2766 or visit www.jacobsandwhitehall.com.

Printed in the United States of America

Published in 2022

ISBN: 978-1-946481-75-7

Disclaimer

This publication is intended to be used for educational purposes only. No legal advice is being given, and no attorney-client relationship is intended to be created by reading this material. The author assumes no liability for any errors or omissions, for how this book or its contents are used or interpreted, or for any consequences resulting directly or indirectly from the use of this book. For legal or any other advice, please consult with an experienced attorney who is aware of the specific facts of your case.

Huff Law, PLC

(757) 394.3434
www.hufflawplc.com

Newport News Office
11815 Fountain Way, Suite 300
Newport News, VA 23606

Virginia Beach Office
780 Lynnhaven Parkway, Suite 400
Virginia Beach, VA 23452

Testimonials

"Always positive and friendly, Ekaterina Huff did an amazing job with our marriage-based green card application!!! We were provided with specific details on the documentation we needed to provide for the case and once confident we had a solid application, Ekaterina was instrumental in the submission process. Ekaterina responded to any questions during the application process immediately and the advice given was always extremely informative. We would thoroughly and without hesitation recommend hiring Ekaterina for anyone seeking a marriage-based residence."

– Simon B.

****

"Ekaterina Huff helped us with the whole process of becoming a permanent resident through marriage. She was very professional and guided us step by step, explaining every piece of paper that we needed for the application with USCIS. Would highly recommend her service."

– Aleksandar

****

"Ekaterina helped me a lot with my case. Immigration sent me a denial later and she turned the case around and now I have my green card. Strongly recommend to anyone."

– Simon

****

"Ekaterina Huff is the best immigration lawyer around! She did an amazing job. Fast, informative, and most importantly, caring. Highly recommended!"

– Svetlana L.

****

"What can I say about Ekaterina Huff…one of the best things that's happened to me in the city! The best lawyer in town. Very smart, open-minded, and creative. Always gives you the feeling that she is more than just a lawyer. Highly recommended. 10 Stars from me."

– Youness T.

****

TABLE OF CONTENTS

i. **Testimonials** **4**

ii. **About The Author** **8**

1. **What Is A Green Card?** **15**

2. **Applying For A Marriage-Based Green Card** **18**

3. **Key Documents Needed To Prove A Bona Fide Marriage** **28**

4. **Misconceptions About The Marriage-Based Green Card Interview** **39**

5. **Preparing For The Marriage-Based Green Card Interview** **49**

6. **Success On The Interview Day** **57**

7. **Possible Outcomes Of A Marriage-Based Green Card Interview** 69

8. **Should I Hire An Immigration Lawyer For A Marriage-Based Green Card Case?** 73

iii. **Notices** 81

iv. **Notes** 94

About The Author

My name is Ekaterina ("Kate") B. Huff and I am a United States immigration attorney in Virginia. I was born and raised in Russia. There, I received my law degree from Volgograd State University, practiced law, and eventually decided to move to the United States. While in the United States, I knew I wanted to continue practicing law. I also met my husband. I had to personally go through the marriage-based green card process with my husband. While in that process, I decided that this is what I wanted to do – help others navigate through this tough time.

I received my law degree from William and Mary Law School. I am licensed to practice law in Washington D.C. I only practice immigration law. Immigration law is federal law and not state law. Because immigration law is federal law, I am able to handle immigration cases from any state or country in the world.

I concentrate my practice primarily on family-based immigration matters, which is a niche area of immigration law. Family-based immigration matters include marriage-based green cards, which is one of the most popular types of green card cases. Marriage-based green cards are especially popular where I am located because of the vast amount of military bases nearby and the amount of military personnel finding love overseas.

Because my practice is heavily focused on marriage-based green card cases, I have handled the full spectrum of marriage-based green card cases ranging from:

- Marriages that were arranged by third parties;
- Marriages with a significant age difference between the couple;
- Marriages with a couple that does not speak a common language;
- Marriages with a couple that has a vast difference in their cultural and ethnic backgrounds;
- Marriages with a couple whose family and friends are unaware of their marriage;
- Marriages with a couple that has not lived together since getting married;
- Marriages where the foreign national spouse is a friend of the U.S. citizen or U.S. green card holder spouse's family;
- Marriages where a couple has made discrepancies in answers to questions at a green card interview they should have mutually known;
- Marriages that were entered into immediately following a foreign national spouse's "Apprehension or Departure Order"; and

- Marriages where the U.S. citizen or U.S. green card holder spouse has filed a previous Immigration petition for a previous foreign national spouse.

Interestingly, I have noticed that a lot of immigration attorneys themselves are foreign nationals or otherwise come from a non-American background. However, a majority of them are second or third generation immigrants, meaning that they did not migrate to the United States from a foreign country, but instead their parents or grandparents did. And if they are a first generation immigrant, they likely came to the United States as a small child.

What makes me different is that I am a first generation immigrant that came to the United States when I was 20 years old. I still have vivid memories of the immigration process that I had to personally endure.

My journey is that I originally came to the United States on a non-immigrant J-1 visa, which is a work and travel visa. After that, I changed my immigration status to a non-immigrant F-1 visa, which is a student visa. After that, I married my husband who is a U.S. citizen and I immediately applied for a marriage-based green card. That process included a marriage-based green card interview.

During my green card interview, my husband and I were separated and questioned separately by an overzealous immigration officer. Nonetheless, I was able to obtain my "2-year conditional greencard," which is a green card given to a foreign national spouse that has been married for less than two years at the time of the green card approval.

Prior to my 2-year conditional greencard expiring, I applied to remove my "conditions on residence" so that I could obtain my "10-year permanent greencard," which is a green card given to a foreign national spouse that has been married for two years or more at the time of the green card approval.

To do this, I filed a Form I-751, Petition To Remove Conditions On Residence. This process required my husband and I to attend another marriage-based green card interview. Afterwards, I was able to obtain my 10-year permanent green card.

After having had a green card in total for three years, I applied for U.S. citizenship, where I had to once again present evidence of my marriage, attend a naturalization interview, and take a mandatory civic exam. Afterwards, I passed the civic exam and was able to obtain my U.S. citizenship.

Lastly, when my parents in Russia were ready to move to the United States, I petitioned for them to obtain a parent-based green card based on them being a parent of a U.S. citizen who is at least 21 years old. As a result, my mother and father were able to obtain their green cards simply based on the fact that I am their daughter and am a U.S. citizen that is at least 21 years old.

In all, my personal experience, education, and professional experience allow me to successfully navigate this process from start to finish. I have handled hundreds of these cases. When my clients come to me, I can relate to them personally and professionally. I can understand all of their questions, concerns, emotions, and even their frustrations.

This is my passion.

Who Is This Book For?

This book is for any couple going through the process of obtaining a green card in the United States based on their marriage. I wanted to write this book to discuss the marriage-based green card process because it is lengthy, complex, and stressful.

CHAPTER 1

WHAT IS A GREEN CARD?

A "green card" is the official document that allows a foreign national person to lawfully live and work in the United States. A green card is formally called a "permanent resident card." In the United States, there are several ways to obtain a green card. You can obtain a green card:

- Through your family members;
- Through your employment;

- By having refugee or asylee status;
- By being a "special immigrant";
- By being a victim of human trafficking or a serious crime;
- Under the Violence Against Women Act ("VAWA") (which also applies to any gender), by being a victim of physical abuse or extreme cruelty from an "immediate relative" that is a U.S. citizen or a U.S. green card holder; and
- By winning the diversity visa (lottery) program.

With that being said, my practice is concentrated on helping people obtain a green card through their family members. If you want to obtain a green card through a family member, you should know that there are five subcategories of family-based green cards that you may be eligible for. Specifically, you can obtain a family-based green card if you are:

1. A U.S. citizen's immediate relative. An "immediate relative" is a spouse, a parent, or an unmarried child that is under 21 years old;

2. An "other family member" based on a "preference system":

- F1 preference category - A U.S. citizen's unmarried child that is 21 years old or older.
- F2a preference category - A U.S. green card holder's spouse or unmarried child that is under 21 years old.
- F2b preference category - A U.S. green card holder's unmarried child that is 21 years old or older.
- F3 preference category - A U.S. citizen's married child.
- F4 preference category - A U.S. citizen's sibling.

3. A U.S. citizen's fiancé;
4. A U.S. citizen's widow(er);
5. A "VAWA" self-petitioner due to being a victim of physical abuse or extreme cruelty from an immediate relative that is a U.S. citizen or a U.S. green card holder.

CHAPTER 2

APPLYING FOR A MARRIAGE-BASED GREEN CARD

A "marriage-based" green card is simply a specific type of family-based green card a foreign national person can obtain.

Any foreign national person that is married to either a U.S. citizen ("USC") or a U.S. green card holder (which is formally called a "lawful permanent resident" or "LPR") can apply for a marriage-based green card in the United States as long as the foreign national person was lawfully admitted to the United States. In this type of green card case, the foreign national person will obtain a green card based solely on the fact that he or she is married to a USC or LPR.

In a marriage-based green card case, the USC or LPR spouse is called the "Petitioner" and the foreign national spouse is called the "Beneficiary" or "Applicant." The immigration Forms you are required to complete in a marriage-based green card case will refer to each spouse using those aforementioned terms.

A marriage-based green card applies to all types of couples that get married. This includes same-sex couples, couples with a significant age difference, couples that met each other years ago, and couples that met each other recently, etc.

The main thing to understand is that the marriage-based green card process, including the green card interview, involves both spouses in the marriage. This means that the USC or LPR spouse is required to participate in the entire green card process along with the foreign national spouse.

How Long After Getting Married Does My Spouse And I Have To Wait To Apply For A Marriage-Based Green Card?

There is no wait-time to apply for a marriage-based green card after getting married. Likewise, there is no deadline to apply for a marriage-based green card after getting married. Therefore, it is entirely up to you when to apply for a marriage-based green card.

You could literally apply for a marriage-based green card the day after you get married. Just keep in mind that it takes time to gather all of the evidence and complete the required immigration Forms. You never want to rush when it comes to preparing a marriage-based green card application because a poorly prepared application will undoubtedly create a long and rocky road ahead.

Ways To Apply For A Marriage-Based Green Card

There are two ways to apply for a marriage-based green card in the United States. The method chosen depends on whether the foreign national spouse is physically located inside or outside the United States at the time of applying for a green card:

1. **If the foreign national spouse is inside the United States -** Your marriage-based green card application must be filed with the United States Citizenship and Immigration Services ("USCIS"). You will be required to complete and file immigration Forms: I-130/I-130A, I-485, I-864, I-765 and I-131. These forms can be filed simultaneously. Notably, the foreign national spouse cannot receive a marriage-based green card unless and until USCIS first approves the Form I-130. The Form I-765 is not technically required, but it is recommended if the foreign national spouse would like to be able to legally

work in the United States while his or her green card case is pending. Moreover, the Form I-131 is not technically required, but it is recommended if the foreign national spouse would like to be able to legally leave and re-enter the United States while his or her green card case is pending. There will be a green card interview at the end of the process that will take place at your local USCIS Field Office. Both spouses are required to attend the green card interview. After the green card interview is over and if the green card application has been approved, the foreign national spouse will receive his or her actual green card in the mail.

2. **If the foreign national spouse is outside the United States -** Your marriage-based green card application will be filed in two stages. The first stage is that you will be required to complete and file immigration Form I-130/I-130A with the United States Citizenship and Immigration Services ("USCIS"). Notably, the foreign national spouse cannot move on to the second stage unless

and until USCIS first approves the Form I-130. If the Form I-130 is approved by USCIS, your case will move on to the second stage. The second stage is that your case will be transferred from USCIS to the National Visa Center ("NVC"). NVC will collect your civil documents, affidavit of support, immigrant visa application, and application fees. Once the above-mentioned documents have been received and reviewed by NVC, it will then transfer your case to the U.S. Embassy in the foreign national spouse's country of residence. There will be a green card interview at the end of the process that will take place at the U.S. Embassy in the foreign national spouse's country of residence. Only the foreign national spouse is required to attend the green card interview. The USC or LPR spouse is not required to attend the green card interview. After the green card interview is over and if the green card application has been approved, the foreign national spouse will receive a visa that allows him or her to enter the United States. After the foreign national spouse enters the United States using that visa, he or she will receive his or her actual green card in the mail.

What Is The Typical Timeframe For A Marriage-Based Green Card Case?

The typical timeframe for a marriage-based green card case ranges from 6 - 18 months.

This timeframe starts on the date you mail your marriage-based green card application to USCIS and it ends on the date you receive your approval or denial letter from USCIS or the U.S. Embassy. The marriage-based green card interview is the last step in the process prior to you receiving an approval or denial letter from USCIS or the U.S. Embassy.

It should be noted that this book is primarily focused on acing a green card interview that takes place at a USCIS Field Office, not a U.S. Embassy. Therefore, this book mainly applies to couples with a foreign national spouse that is physically located inside the United States and, thus, will have a green card interview at a USCIS Field Office. Nevertheless, the information contained in this book is still helpful to a foreign national spouse that is physically located outside the United States and, thus, will have a green card interview at a U.S. Embassy.

In order to start the marriage-based green card process when a foreign national spouse is in the United States, you must first get legally married, gather and collect the evidence needed to prove a bona fide marriage (i.e., a real and loving marriage), prepare and file all of the required personal documents with USCIS, and prepare and file all of the required immigration Forms with USCIS. This includes, but is not limited to, filing immigration Forms: I-130/I-130A, I-485, I-864, I-765 and I-131.

Next, you will receive in the mail various confirmation "Notices of Receipt" from USCIS advising you that they have received your marriage-based green card application. (*See* pages 82 - 85).

After that, you will receive in the mail a "Notice of Biometrics Appointment" from USCIS advising of the date and time you are required to appear at your local USCIS Field Office to provide your biometric information (e.g., your fingerprints, etc.). (*See* page 86).

After that, you will receive in the mail a "Notice of Approval or Denial" from USCIS, but only for your Application For Employment Authorization (Form I-765) and your Application For Travel Document (Form I-131). (*See* pages 87 - 88).

After that, you will receive in the mail a "Notice of Green Card Interview" from USCIS for your marriage-based green card interview. (*See* page 89). It typically takes 6 - 12 months after the date you have filed your marriage-based green card application to receive an interview notice from USCIS. Now the end is finally in sight!

Then, you and your spouse will appear at your local USCIS Field Office for your marriage-based green card interview. Your green card interview will be your first time dealing with someone physically in front of you. This can be very intimidating — especially when you are dealing with the federal government. In fact, I have learned in my practice that a lot of my clients feel the interview is the most intimidating part of the process, which is why I have decided to write this book.

Lastly, you will receive in the mail a "Notice of Approval or Denial" from USCIS for your Petition For Alien Relative (Form I-130) and your Application To Register Permanent Residence Or Adjust Status (Form I-485). (*See* pages 91 - 92). If your case was approved, you will soon receive in the mail your actual green card. (*See* page 93).

Chapter 3

Key Documents Needed To Prove A Bona Fide Marriage

USCIS will approve your marriage-based green card application — specifically your Form I-130 —only if it finds that you and your spouse entered into a valid marriage and have a bona fide marriage. Notably, there is a difference between a "valid marriage" and a "bona fide marriage."

A marriage is considered "valid" if it is a legal marriage where it takes place, unless it violates U.S. public policy (for example, a marriage between family members or a polygamous marriage). Whereas a marriage is considered "bona fide" if it is an honest marriage that was entered into in "good faith."

Therefore, a "bona fide marriage" is a marriage where each spouse genuinely loves each other and intends to share a life with each other. Simply put, it means it's a real and loving marriage. The important thing is the couple's intentions at the time they enter into the marriage, even if that marriage later breaks up.

Typically, a bona fide marriage must be proven by a "preponderance of evidence" standard. That standard requires the USC or LPR spouse to prove that "it is more likely than not" the marriage is a real and loving marriage. However, if a USC or LPR marries a foreign national person while the foreign national person is in removal (i.e., deportation) proceedings, the USC or LPR spouse must now prove by "clear and convincing evidence" that the marriage is a real and loving marriage.

USCIS lists on their website the evidence you need to submit with your marriage-based green card application in order to prove that you have a bona fide marriage. You can see that list by visiting this website: https://www.uscis.gov/i-130. Notice that their list is somewhat vague.

Therefore, I always tell my clients that there are 3 Tiers of evidence that you should submit with a marriage-based green card application in order to prove a bona fide marriage. The tiers vary depending on their level of importance and persuasiveness to USCIS. Tier 1 is the most important whereas Tier 3 is the least important.

Tier 1 evidence consists of documents that prove you and your spouse have a deeply-intertwined life together. This includes evidence that you and your spouse have a child together or commingle finances. To be clear, having a child with a USC or LPR spouse is not a requirement for a foreign national spouse to obtain a green card, but it is certainly persuasive to USCIS that a couple is in a real and loving marriage. The best example of a document that proves you and your spouse have a child together is a birth certificate listing you and your spouse as the mother and father. Furthermore, joint financial documents are important to USCIS because a real and loving couple will usually mix or combine their income and debts to some degree. Examples of documents that prove you and your spouse commingle finances are: (i) joint checking and/or savings bank account statements that show an active transaction history by both spouses; (ii) joint credit and/or debit card statements that show an active transaction history by both spouses; (iii) a joint lease or mortgage; and (iv) joint tax returns.

Tier 2 evidence consists of documents that prove you and your spouse have a shared life together. Documents that show a shared life together are important to USCIS because a real and loving couple will usually obtain joint insurance policies and split responsibilities like paying bills. These documents are essentially the same as the Tier 1 documents, but on a smaller scale. Examples of documents that prove you and your spouse have a shared life together are: (i) a joint health insurance and/or dental insurance plan; (ii) a joint automobile insurance plan; (iii) a joint cell phone plan; and (iv) joint utility bills.

Tier 3 evidence consists of documents that prove you and your spouse are a real and loving couple. Documents that show the couple is a real and loving couple are important to USCIS because a real and loving couple will usually memorialize their relationship and preserve their memories. Standing alone, the evidence in this tier is not sufficient to prove that you have a bona fide marriage. Rather this evidence is more like the cherry on top – but it is not going to do the job by itself. Examples of documents that prove you and your spouse are a real and loving couple are: (i) pictures taken throughout various points in the relationship of you and your spouse together while alone and also with friends and family;

(ii) birthday, holiday, and anniversary cards from one spouse to another; (iii) wedding invitations to your wedding; (iv) mail received listing the name of both spouses at the same address; (v) a joint gym membership or joint membership to wholesale warehouses (Costco, Sam's Club, BJ's, etc.); and (vi) notarized affidavits from friends, family members, co-workers, and neighbors that attest under oath to the real and loving relationship that you and your spouse have.

Even if you do not have many of these documents in the beginning of your case when you file your marriage-based green card application with USCIS, you can simply bring these documents to your green card interview and hand it to the USCIS officer at your interview. After all, it typically takes 6 - 12 months after the date you have filed your marriage-based green card application to receive an interview notice from USCIS. This means that you will have 6 - 12 months after you have filed your application to obtain the evidence needed to prove that you have a bona fide marriage. However, it is best to be proactive and file substantial evidence upfront with your green card application. This will make your green card interview go much, much smoother.

Will USCIS Ask My Spouse To Show That He Or She Will Support Me?

A marriage-based green card application must include evidence that the USC or LPR spouse will be able to adequately support the foreign national spouse.

When USCIS mentions "supporting" the foreign national spouse, it does not mean that the USC or LPR spouse must buy their groceries and pay for their clothes. Instead, it means that the foreign national spouse will not be eligible to obtain certain public assistance benefits offered by the U.S. government, such as welfare and food stamps. Because of this, USCIS wants to see evidence that the USC or LPR spouse can adequately provide for the foreign national spouse. As a result, USCIS wants to know how much money the USC or LPR spouse makes in order to confirm that he or she can adequately support the foreign national spouse.

In the event that the foreign national spouse does receive public assistance benefits offered by the U.S. government, the petitioning USC or LPR spouse may be required to pay it back.

With that being said, the USC or LPR spouse must file an immigration Form I-864, which is an Affidavit of Support under Section 213A of the INA. That Form is essentially a contract between the USC or LPR spouse and the U.S. government stating that the foreign national spouse will not apply for any public assistance benefits offered by the U.S. government. The USC or LPR spouse must file the Form I-864 simultaneously with the marriage-based green card application. The USC or LPR spouse must provide his or her most recent tax returns along with the Form I-864.

In order to adequately support a foreign national spouse, the USC or LPR spouse must make an annual income of 125% of the poverty guidelines relative to their household size (or 100% of the poverty guidelines relative to their household size if the USC or LPR spouse is in the military). You can see the poverty guidelines by visiting this website: https://www.uscis.gov/i-864p.

If the USC or LPR spouse does not make the annual income amount required by the poverty guidelines, you can include income from a "financial co-sponsor." The financial co-sponsor will need to adequately ensure to USCIS that the foreign national spouse will not apply for any public assistance benefits offered by the U.S. government. The financial co-sponsor can be any person that is a U.S. citizen or a U.S. green card holder. Notably, the income of the USC or LPR spouse cannot be combined with the income of the financial co-sponsor. This means that the income of the financial co-sponsor will be considered by itself and, thus, the financial co-sponsor will have to personally meet the poverty guidelines. Therefore, the financial co-sponsor will be required to file his or her own Form

I-864 and provide his or her most recent tax returns. The financial co-sponsor must make an annual income of 125% of the poverty guidelines relative to their household size (even if the financial co-sponsor is in the military). In the alternative, if the USC or LPR spouse does not make the annual income amount required by the poverty guidelines, you can include income from a "household member" by filing a Form I-864A in addition to filing a Form I-864. A "household member" for purposes of the Form I-864A is:

- The foreign national spouse that is intending to obtain a marriage-based green card;
- A parent, adult son or daughter, or sibling with the same principal residence as the USC or LPR spouse; and
- Any person who the USC or LPR spouse lawfully claimed as a dependent on their most recent federal tax returns even if that person does not share the same principal residence as the USC or LPR spouse.

Notably, unlike when a financial co-sponsor is used, the income of the USC or LPR spouse will be combined with the income of the household member.

Moreover, if the USC or LPR spouse, financial co-sponsor, or household member is unable to provide to USCIS their tax returns for the most recent tax year, he or she must provide to USCIS a tax extension request with the IRS, their most recent tax returns, and 3 - 6 recent pay stubs that reflect their current income.

I have seen several green card cases get slowed down because of issues with the USC or LPR spouse's income. It is always best to determine upfront if you will need to use a financial co-sponsor or a household member. This way you can file the financial co-sponsor or household member's documents at the same time you file your marriage-based green card application. This will make your whole green card case go much faster and it will ease your green card interview.

CHAPTER 4

MISCONCEPTIONS ABOUT THE MARRIAGE-BASED GREEN CARD INTERVIEW

The first misconception is that there is not always an interview required for a green card case. This is technically true because USCIS does have the power to waive a green card interview for other types of green card cases, but not for a marriage-based green card case.

The types of green card cases where USCIS can waive a green card interview are cases that involve: (Chapter 5A of USCIS Policy Manual)

- A foreign national person who is clearly ineligible;
- A foreign national unmarried child of a USC where the unmarried child is under 21 years old and has filed with USCIS a Form I-485 on their own;
- A foreign national parent of a USC;
- A foreign national unmarried child of a LPR where the unmarried child is under 14 years old and has filed with USCIS a Form I-485 on their own;
- A USC that is in the military;
- A USC that is incarcerated; and
- A USC or foreign national person with an illness that prevents him or her from physically appearing at a USCIS office for an interview.

The purpose of the marriage-based green card interview is twofold:

1. To prove to USCIS that your marriage is a bona fide marriage that was entered into solely for the

purpose of love and unionship and not to fraudulently obtain immigration benefits such as a green card; and

2. To prove to USCIS that you meet all of the eligibility requirements to obtain a green card.

There are obvious reasons for a marriage-based green card interview because, unfortunately, there are people that enter into a sham marriage for the sole purpose of obtaining a green card. Therefore, the USCIS officer will scrutinize your marriage in order to determine if your marriage was in fact entered into in good faith solely for the purpose of love and unionship and not to fraudulently obtain immigration benefits such as a green card.

The second misconception is that the green card interview will be a very easy and straightforward process. This couldn't be further from the truth. In particular, I have learned that many couples feel confident that their interview will be a very easy and straightforward process since their marriage is a real and loving marriage that was entered into solely for the purpose of love and unionship. The problem, however, is that nervousness and intimidation can quickly take control. An otherwise straightforward case may quickly turn into an intensely scrutinized interview. This is because your nervousness and intimidation can lead you into saying something that harms your case or opens up a can of worms.

To be clear, the USCIS officer is not there to trick you, but he or she is there to ask you questions to determine if you have a bona fide marriage and if you meet all of the eligibility requirements to obtain a green card. I have seen couples start to panic when the USCIS officer asks them a question in a pessimistic tone of voice or when the USCIS officer phrases a question in a way that the couple may not fully understand. Sometimes it is simply the timing of the question that may throw the couple off.

When you panic, you make senseless mistakes and forget vital information during the interview such as your spouse's birth date or your spouse's mother's name, etc. This raises an eyebrow and causes scrutinizing questions to arise. Even a minor mistake can throw off your whole interview.

The third misconception is that the USCIS officer will scrutinize your marriage depending on the amount of time you waited to apply for a green card after getting married. For the most part, couples that apply for a green card do not wait several years after getting married to do so. They usually do it right away. This is because the foreign national spouse is usually eager to establish a permanent residency. This is especially true if the foreign national spouse does not currently have any legal immigration status in the United States. For the foreign national spouse, obtaining a green card equals more opportunities in the United States. This is because a green card allows the foreign national spouse to lawfully live and work in the United States and become a productive member of society. It is your golden ticket. USCIS understands this.

Typically, when couples get married, the foreign national spouse will usually apply for a green card soon after getting married to the USC or LPR spouse. I have seen couples apply for a green card the day after getting married, a few months after getting married, and even a few years after getting married. I have also seen the rare cases where couples apply for a green card 10 years or more after getting married. If a couple does not apply for a green card right away, it is usually because of financial reasons. It does cost money to file for a green card and the fees to USCIS are high, and they keep getting higher.

Another common situation where I have seen couples wait many years after getting married to apply for a green card is with military couples that have lived overseas for an extended period of time. This is a situation where a USC spouse is in the military and is stationed overseas. The USC spouse would meet their foreign national spouse overseas and remain living with their foreign national spouse overseas while serving in the military. During this timeframe, the foreign national spouse has no reason or incentive to apply for a green card in the United States. Then at some point, the USC spouse retires or gets stationed back in the United States and the foreign national spouse is now ready to apply for a green card.

Regardless of how long you wait to apply for a marriage-based green card, USCIS understands that the dynamic and circumstances of every marriage is different. Therefore, the level of scrutiny your case will get really depends on your particular USCIS officer and the overall strength of the evidence you have submitted with your green card application.

I have learned that the stronger the evidence is that you submit upfront with your green card application, the easier your interview will go.

Realistic Concerns My Spouse And I Should Have Heading Into A Marriage-Based Green Card Interview

Each case is different and comes with its own individual problems and hurdles. No couples are alike, and no marriages are alike. Ultimately, in a marriage-based green card interview, USCIS is looking for (1) evidence that your marriage was entered into solely for the purpose of love and unionship and not to fraudulently obtain immigration benefits such as a green card. This is called being in a bona fide marriage; and (2) evidence that you meet all of the eligibility requirements to obtain a green card.

With that being said, you should be concerned with simply satisfying both of those prongs. I have seen USCIS officers red-flag certain types of marriage-based green card cases. Once red-flagged, a case will receive extra scrutiny and questioning from USCIS. The cases that get red-flagged usually involve couples that do not have the strongest evidence of a bona fide marriage, couples with a significant age difference, couples that have been married several times before their current marriage, and couples where the foreign national spouse has a criminal conviction on his or her criminal record. I have also noticed that many same-sex couples receive extra scrutiny and questioning from USCIS because, although legal, same-sex marriages have become a new way for people to obtain green cards fraudulently. Same-sex couples are not treated differently, but their marriage may be given more scrutiny.

During the green card interview, the USCIS officer will undoubtedly scrutinize and question any problem areas or weaknesses in your case. To avoid having any problems during the green card interview, you should be proactive and file substantial evidence upfront with your green card application.

To do this, you should gather and accumulate as much evidence as possible of having a bona fide marriage. In addition, you should identify any problem areas or weaknesses in your case. Once identified, you should then take proactive steps to prove to USCIS that the problem area or weakness in your case does not invalidate the legitimacy of your marriage or otherwise make the foreign national spouse ineligible to obtain a green card. You must address every problem area or weakness in your case by providing explanatory evidence to USCIS. Most importantly, you should be proactive and file this evidence upfront with your green card application instead of waiting to file it at your green card interview. However, you should proceed with caution and ensure not to volunteer too much information to USCIS, as that could open new doors for scrutiny.

Do Couples Sometimes Underestimate The Marriage-Based Green Card Interview?

Couples frequently underestimate the marriage-based green card interview. The main thing to remember is that USCIS officers are human. They experience different emotions and make mistakes. Sometimes the USCIS officer is having a bad day or interviewed a tough couple right before your interview. So if you catch the USCIS officer on a bad day, your interview could be bad. The USCIS officer's mood may cause him or her to find more weaknesses in your case. Plus, some USCIS officers are naturally more strict than others. In my practice, I have noticed that the best time for an interview is after 1:00pm. This is because the USCIS officers have had their lunch break and their work day is almost over. Unfortunately, couples do not have any control over the date and time of their marriage-based green card interview.

CHAPTER 5

PREPARING FOR THE MARRIAGE-BASED GREEN CARD INTERVIEW

It typically takes 6 - 12 months after the date you have filed your marriage-based green card application to have your green card interview.

First and foremost, the best way to prepare for a marriage-based green card interview is to bring a copy of your entire green card application with you to your interview. Your "entire green card application" means all immigration Forms and supporting evidence you have filed with USCIS.

The key is to make sure that the verbal answers you give to the USCIS officer during your green card interview matches everything you wrote in your green card application.

Typically, when the USCIS officer interviews you, he or she will go through your entire green card application while sitting in front of you. Sometimes the USCIS officer will ask you questions related to your application, but not related to your marriage. This usually happens when a couple has been married for over two years, has a child together, or has submitted an overwhelming amount of evidence of a bona fide marriage upfront with their application.

Regardless, the best way to make your interview go as easy as possible is to file substantial evidence of a bona fide marriage upfront with your application. Even if you do that, you will still be required to provide the USCIS officer at your interview with the original version of all evidence you have filed with your application.

At the beginning or end of the interview, the USCIS officer will typically ask if there is anything else you would like to add to your application before he or she makes a decision. This is the point in time where you should provide to the USCIS officer any personal documents or evidence that you have failed to provide upfront with your application. This is also the point in time where you should provide to the USCIS officer any new evidence that proves you are in a real and loving marriage. This is particularly important if you applied for a marriage-based green card immediately after getting married. This is because you may not have filed with your application the full scope of evidence the USCIS officer wants to see. Therefore, the USCIS officer will expect you to bring more evidence of a bona fide marriage to your interview.

Your interview will be recorded, so be careful what you say even when your USCIS officer steps out of the room. The recording can be reviewed and transcribed by the USCIS officer after the interview is over.

Once Immigration Has Reviewed Our Marriage-Based Green Card Application, Where Does The Interview Take Place?

When you file your marriage-based green card application, you must mail it to either a USCIS Lockbox Facility or a USCIS Service Center. You can see exactly where you need to mail your application by visiting this website:

https://www.uscis.gov/forms/all-forms/direct-filing-addresses-for-form-i-485-application-to-register-permanent-residence-or-adjust-status.

Your marriage-based green card interview will take place in-person at your local USCIS Field Office. You cannot have your interview online via video chat. The address where the foreign national spouse resides determines which USCIS Field Office your interview will take place.

Will Both Spouses Attend One Interview?

Usually both spouses are required to simultaneously attend one marriage-based green card interview together. So if you are sitting in the waiting room and the USCIS officer comes out for just one of you, you are probably in trouble. A standard marriage-based green card interview should start with both spouses present at the same time. However, if something happens during the interview that makes the USCIS officer doubt the accuracy of the spouses' answers or intentions, the spouses can be separated. If that happens, one spouse will be asked to stay in the interview room and the other spouse will be moved to a different interview room or the waiting room. The USCIS officer will ask each spouse questions separately regarding specific topics and then compare their answers to see if they line up with each other.

Will There Be Separate USCIS Officers Conducting The Interview If My Spouse And I Get Separated?

There is typically only one USCIS officer conducting the marriage-based green card interview. Even if you and your spouse are separated during the interview, there will typically be only one USCIS officer conducting both interviews.

I have, however, seen interviews where there were two USCIS officers present. I have seen this happen when a couple was together and also when a couple was separated. It really depends on the underlying issues in the specific case. Frankly, there is no good reason for two USCIS officers to be there, unless one of them is in training. When a second USCIS officer is present, that second officer is usually the Field Director of the USCIS Field Office (which is the top USCIS officer in that office) or a lower level supervisor. This could be a bad sign, but not always.

Though, there are times when a second USCIS officer will pop in to your interview solely to witness the answers you give to the interviewing USCIS officer's questions and to certify in writing that they have "witnessed your answer."

Who Are These USCIS Officers?

The USCIS officer conducting your marriage-based green card interview is a federal government employee that works for the U.S. Citizenship and Immigration Services ("USCIS"), which is an agency of the U.S. Department of Homeland Security ("DHS") that administers the country's naturalization and overseas lawful immigration to the United States.

Each USCIS officer has a Policy Manual, which is essentially a handbook of immigration policies and procedures. A well-prepared immigration attorney will have a copy of that Policy Manual and use it to help prepare his or her clients. I always bring that Policy Manual with me to my green card interviews, and if there is an issue, I point it out to the USCIS officer and reference the specific page and paragraph in the Policy Manual that addresses the issue. If there is still an issue after pointing it out to the USCIS officer, the Field Director or a lower level supervisor will pop in to the interview and iron it out. You can see the USCIS Policy Manual by visiting this website:

https://www.uscis.gov/policy-manual/volume-7

CHAPTER 6

SUCCESS ON THE INTERVIEW DAY

I recommend that you retain an experienced immigration attorney to appear with you at your marriage-based green card interview. I recommend you do this even if you choose not to retain an immigration attorney to prepare your underlying marriage-based green card application. An immigration attorney knows the ins and outs of immigration law similar to how a tax attorney knows the ins and outs of tax law.

Will Our Immigration Attorney Be Allowed In The Interview Room?

You have the right to have an immigration attorney with you in the interview room during your marriage-based green card interview. To be clear, there is no "requirement" that you have an immigration attorney with you at the interview, but you certainly have the "right" to have one.

What Information Is Safe To Share With The USCIS Officer During The Interview?

Whether you decide to have an immigration attorney appear with you at your interview or go without one, it is safe to share with the USCIS officer any information and evidence that proves: (1) you are in a bona fide marriage (i.e., a real and loving marriage); and (2) you meet all of the eligibility requirements to obtain a green card.

When you step into the interview room, the first thing you do is swear to tell the truth and nothing but the truth. You cannot lie. If you get caught lying, your marriage-based green card application can be denied. I have seen numerous people distraught over the fact that they were caught lying to USCIS and know that they have been deemed inadmissible (i.e., cannot receive a green card) and will be required to file a Waiver of Inadmissibility.

The biggest thing to remember is that your marriage-based green card application and supporting evidence probably totals over 200 sheets of paper. The USCIS officer will have all of that paperwork in front of him or her during your interview. It is very important that the verbal answers you give during your interview matches all of that paperwork.

Technically speaking, you have the right to not answer a question you believe will jeopardize your application. However, this is a double-edged sword because if you refuse to answer a question, that will absolutely give rise to suspicion.

Key Dates And Events In Our Relationship The USCIS Officer Will Likely Ask About During The Interview

The USCIS officer will typically ask you about key dates in your relationship. I have seen USCIS officers ask my clients about the dates the couple met, got proposed to, and had their wedding. So it may be important for you to have those major dates memorized. After all, a real and loving couple would naturally remember those dates.

Even if the USCIS officer does not ask you about key dates in your relationship, he or she may ask you and your spouse about each other's birth date, etc. The USCIS officer may ask about mundane and random topics, such as the last movie you and your spouse watched together, the color of the curtains in your living room, and what you and your spouse ate for dinner last night. Those questions are designed to see if you and your spouse are in fact a real and loving couple.

Moreover, a major portion of the interview will be dedicated to making sure that all of the information in your green card application is correct. The USCIS officer may ask you questions about any inconsistencies and contradictions in your green card application. This may include questions such as where you and your spouse have lived and worked in the past five years, etc.

What If We Don't Know The Answer To A Question?

If the USCIS officer asks you a question that you do not know the answer to, simply tell the USCIS officer "I do not know."

You are human. There is nothing wrong with being imperfect, making a mistake, or not knowing the answer to a question. The best piece of advice in this situation is to be honest with the USCIS officer. It is better to say "I don't know" than it is to lie and perjure yourself under oath.

The USCIS officer knows that you are human and are likely nervous. The USCIS officer is likely taking all of that into account and will not fault you for it. As long as you do not answer "I don't know" to every question, you will be fine.

What If I Or My Spouse Had A Previous Marriage That Involved Immigration?

The USCIS officer will most likely scrutinize a previous marriage that involved Immigration. This scrutiny will happen regardless of whether the USC or LPR spouse or the foreign national spouse had a previous marriage that involved Immigration.

If any spouse had a previous marriage that involved Immigration, the USCIS officer will look at how recently that previous marriage occurred. If the previous marriage occurred recently, the USCIS officer may have a suspicion that your current marriage is not a real and loving marriage.

Namely, if you are a USC or LPR spouse that has previously married a foreign national person that has applied for some type of immigration benefit, USCIS will have a suspicion that you married your current foreign national spouse in order to help him or her obtain some type of immigration benefit. In other words, you might be viewed as a "career petitioner."

And vice versa. If you are a foreign national spouse that has previously married a USC or LPR and you have previously applied for some type of immigration benefit based on that previous marriage, USCIS will have a suspicion that you married your current USC or LPR spouse in order to obtain some type of immigration benefit.

In fact, I have seen USCIS officers during interviews focus most of their questions on a spouse's previous marriage instead of their current marriage. If the USCIS officer has reason to believe that your previous marriage was not a bona fide marriage and you tried to obtain an immigration benefit based on that previous marriage, your current application will likely be denied. The reason is because you would be apparently "providing fraudulent documents and information to USCIS in order to obtain immigration benefits."

A common situation that receives scrutiny from USCIS is when a foreign national spouse receives a marriage-based green card, divorces the underlying USC or LPR spouse that provided the basis for the marriage-based green card, enters into a new marriage with a foreign national person, and then petitions for the newlywed foreign national person to obtain their own marriage-based green card.

In that situation, if the petitioning foreign national spouse is a LPR at the time he or she petitions for the newlywed foreign national person to obtain their own marriage-based green card <u>and</u> the new marriage occurs within 5 years after the petitioning foreign national spouse received his or her green card, the petitioning foreign national spouse will have to prove by "clear and convincing evidence" that his or her previous marriage to the underlying USC or LPR spouse was not done fraudulently to obtain a green card. <u>INA</u> §204(a)(2)(A).

However, if the petitioning foreign national spouse is a USC at the time he or she petitions for the newlywed foreign national person to obtain their own marriage-based green card, there will not be a higher standard of proof and the case will receive less scrutiny.

Nevertheless, USCIS understands that not every marriage is perfect. In fact, the United States has one of the highest divorce rates in the world. Things happen. Just because you got married, divorced, and then chose to marry someone new, doesn't mean that you are in a fraudulent marriage – but it will certainly raise an eyebrow.

Common Reasons My Spouse and I Would Receive Extra Scrutiny At The Interview

There are 8 common reasons you would receive extra scrutiny from a USCIS officer at a marriage-based green card interview.

The first common reason for extra scrutiny is because you and your spouse do not have enough evidence of a bona fide marriage. This is because

USCIS wants to know if you are in a real and loving marriage considering the fact that people in love usually have evidence of a shared life together.

The second common reason for extra scrutiny is because you and your spouse have a significant age difference. This is because USCIS wants to know if you are in a real and loving marriage considering the significant age difference and apparent lack of compatibility.

The third common reason for extra scrutiny is because you and your spouse had your marriage arranged by a third party. This is because USCIS wants to know if you are in a real and loving marriage considering you used a third party to arrange your relationship and marriage.

The fourth common reason for extra scrutiny is because you and your spouse got married soon after meeting each other. This is because USCIS wants to know if you are in a real and loving marriage considering the short timeframe you knew your spouse prior to getting married.

The fifth common reason for extra scrutiny is because you and your spouse do not speak the same language. This is because USCIS wants to know if you are in a real and loving marriage considering you and your spouse are unable to communicate with each other.

The sixth common reason for extra scrutiny is because you and your spouse have not lived together in the same home since getting married. This is because USCIS wants to know if you are in a real and loving marriage considering the fact that married people usually live together in the same home.

The seventh common reason for extra scrutiny is because you or your spouse had a prior marriage that involved Immigration. This is because USCIS wants to know if you are in a real and loving marriage considering you or your spouse had previously filed for, or received, an immigration benefit based on a prior marriage.

The eighth common reason for extra scrutiny is simply by having a tough USCIS officer. The difficulty of your interview very much depends on the USCIS officer you are sitting in front of. Some are more tough than others.

CHAPTER 7

POSSIBLE OUTCOMES OF A MARRIAGE-BASED GREEN CARD INTERVIEW

Usually, the USCIS officer will not outright tell you how you did at the end of your marriage-based green card interview.

Instead, the USCIS officer will usually hand you a paper telling you what to expect next. (*See* page 90). That paper will say: "We have completed your interview. USCIS is unable to complete your case at this time. Your case is being held until a final decision can be made."

Do not worry. This is normal.

There are three ways that this paper can be interpreted:

1. The USCIS officer will approve your case. You will receive your green card in the mail within the next 7-10 calendar days. This happens when your green card interview went well and the USCIS officer does not have any requests for additional evidence.
2. You will receive a "Request For Additional Evidence" ("RFE") in the mail from USCIS within the next 7-10 calendar days. The RFE will tell you the specific additional evidence you will need to provide to USCIS. This could be something as simple as providing updated tax information for the USC or LPR spouse or providing an updated medical exam for the foreign national spouse, etc. Once the USCIS officer receives the additional

evidence from you, he or she will review it to ensure it is sufficient. If your additional evidence is insufficient, the USCIS officer will deny your case. On the other hand, if your additional evidence is sufficient, the USCIS officer will approve your case. Then, you will receive your green card in the mail within the next 7-10 calendar days.

3. You will receive a "Notice of Intent to Deny" ("NOID") in the mail from USCIS within the next 7-10 calendar days. The NOID will tell you the specific reason USCIS is planning to deny your case. You will be given the opportunity to respond to the NOID. If your response to the NOID is insufficient, the USCIS officer will deny your case. On the other hand, if your response to the NOID is sufficient, the USCIS officer will approve your case. Then, you will receive your green card in the mail within the next 7-10 calendar days.

The Most Common Mistake A Couple Makes At An Interview

The most common mistake a couple makes at a marriage-based green card interview is not having enough evidence that they are in a real and loving marriage. This mistake will cause the case to either get delayed by a few months or get denied.

CHAPTER 8

SHOULD I HIRE AN IMMIGRATION LAWYER FOR A MARRIAGE-BASED GREEN CARD CASE?

It would be wise and prudent to hire an immigration attorney for your entire marriage-based green card case. However, technically speaking, you are not required to hire an immigration attorney to prepare your marriage-based green card application or to appear with you at your marriage-based green card interview.

However, I would strongly recommend you hire an immigration attorney to prepare your marriage-based green card application and to appear with you at your marriage-based green card interview.

Hiring an immigration attorney to prepare your green card case is a lot like hiring an accountant to prepare your taxes. The idea is that the professional knows all of the fine-print and technicalities in the law that the average person does not.

An immigration attorney knows how to best represent you in front of the federal government. An immigration attorney knows and comprehends all of the complex immigration laws and policies involved in your case. An immigration attorney knows how to prepare a persuasive marriage-based green card application and supporting evidence. An immigration attorney knows how to avoid many of the mistakes people make during a marriage-based green card interview. An immigration attorney knows the USCIS officers at your local USCIS Field Office and how to best approach them.

What Can Our Immigration Attorney Do For Us Before The Interview?

As I have mentioned throughout this book, the best way to have a successful marriage-based green card interview is file substantial evidence upfront with your marriage-based green card application. Your immigration attorney knows how to make this happen.

I also believe that practice makes perfect, which is why I conduct mock interviews with my clients. I am not sure if every immigration attorney does this, but they should. I will set up a mock interview with my clients in my office 1-2 days before their interview. I purposefully time the mock interview to occur within 48 hours of the actual interview. This keeps everything fresh in mind.

I pretend to be a USCIS officer the moment my clients step into my office for their mock interview. I treat them the same way the USCIS officer will treat them during their interview. I question them the same way the USCIS officer will question them during their interview.

I have been to hundreds of interviews and I can say that although each USCIS officer is different, the interview procedure remains the same. The interview procedure is that the USCIS officer will come into the waiting room to call the foreign national spouse's name, walk the couple to the interview room, have the couple swear to tell the truth, and ask the couple questions about their marriage and application. During the mock interview, I will copy that procedure exactly.

After the mock interview is finished, I will review with my clients what they did well and what needs improvement. My goal is to help my clients obtain the best possible outcome of their interview.

I have learned that conducting a mock interview with my clients is very helpful because merely giving them a sample list of interview questions will not psychologically prepare them for the interview experience. Anyone can find a sample list of interview questions on the internet. But going through a mock interview empowers you to feel comfortable during the actual interview. This maximizes your chances of success.

What Can Our Immigration Attorney Do For Us At The Interview?

It is important to understand the role of an immigration attorney at the interview. The main thing to remember is that your immigration attorney is not allowed to answer questions on your behalf at the interview. The answers to the USCIS officer's questions must come directly from you and your spouse. This means that if the USCIS officer asks a question that you and your spouse do not know the answer to, your immigration attorney cannot answer the question for you.

An immigration attorney can, however, keep the interview within the confines of immigration law and the Policy Manual.

First, if the USCIS officer does something or asks you something that is not permitted by the Policy Manual, an immigration attorney can object – on record – to the impropriety and then inform the USCIS officer of his or her impropriety. This will stop the USCIS officer from using information against you that is not allowed to be considered during a marriage-based green card interview. Because of this, an immigration attorney will allow you to receive a fair and proper interview.

Second, an immigration attorney can advise you on the actual immigration laws during your interview. Some USCIS offices will even have a sign posted somewhere that says: "Your attorney is here not to answer questions for you; they are here to advise you on immigration law if needed." There are times when a USCIS officer will ask a couple questions regarding the foreign national spouse's immigration history and future plans to bring other foreign national family members to the United States. Because of this, an immigration attorney will allow you to be fully advised on the immigration laws during the interview in real-time as it happens.

Third, an immigration attorney can clarify certain information in your marriage-based green card application if there is any confusion from the USCIS officer. It is surprising how often a USCIS officer will erroneously request additional evidence from a couple when the USCIS officer already has the requested evidence in his or her possession. Frankly, these mistakes happen because the USCIS officer has a heavy caseload and, because of that, he or she likely did not thoroughly review the couple's application and its supporting evidence before the interview. An immigration attorney will advise the USCIS officer during the interview that he or she is already in possession of the evidence sought. Because of this, an immigration attorney will prevent you from having any unnecessary delays in receiving your approval or denial letter from USCIS.

Lastly, if you and your spouse are separated from each other during the interview, an immigration attorney will be able to stay in the interview room with each spouse. When the interview is over, the immigration attorney will be able to review each spouse's answers and highlight any discrepancies between them. Because of this, an immigration attorney will allow you to properly assess the success of your interview and the likelihood of receiving an approval letter from USCIS.

If you have any questions or concerns about your case, you may call or text me on my office phone at (757) 394-3434 or email me at ehuff@hufflawplc.com.

Notices

The following Notices are examples of the same Notices that you will receive after you have filed your marriage-based green card application. The Notices are listed in the same order that you will receive them.

1st) Notice of Receipt For Form I-130, Petition For Alien Relative

Department of Homeland Security
U.S. Citizenship and Immigration Services

Form I-797C, Notice of Action

THIS NOTICE DOES NOT GRANT ANY IMMIGRATION STATUS OR BENEFIT.

NOTICE TYPE		NOTICE DATE
Receipt		February 11, 2022
CASE TYPE		USCIS ALIEN NUMBER
I-130, Petition for Alien Relative		
RECEIPT NUMBER	RECEIVED DATE	PAGE
[redacted]	February 09, 2022	1 of 1
PRIORITY DATE	PREFERENCE CLASSIFICATION	DATE OF BIRTH
February 09, 2022	201 B INA SPOUSE OF USC	[redacted]

[redacted]
C/O EKATERINA HUFF HUFF LAW PLC 8 00002114
11815 FOUNTAIN WAY STE 300
NEWPORT NEWS, VA 23606

APPLICANT/PETITIONER NAME AND MAILING ADDRESS

PAYMENT INFORMATION:

Application/Petition Fee:	$535.00
Total Amount Received:	$535.00
Total Balance Due:	$0.00

We have received your form and are currently processing the above case for the following beneficiaries:

Name	Date of Birth	Country of Birth	Class (If Applicable)
[redacted]	[redacted]	[redacted]	

If this notice contains a priority date, this priority does not reflect earlier retained priority dates. We will notify you separately about any other case you filed.

If we determine you must submit biometrics, we will mail you a biometrics appointment notice with the time and place of your appointment.

If you have questions or need to update your personal information listed above, please visit the USCIS Contact Center webpage at uscis.gov/contactcenter to connect with a live USCIS representative in English or Spanish.

USCIS Office Address:
USCIS
National Benefits Center
P.O. Box 648003
Lee's Summit, MO 64002

USCIS Contact Center Number:
(800)375-5283
ATTORNEY COPY

[redacted]

If this is an interview or biometrics appointment notice, please see the back of this notice for important information. Form I-797C 04/01/19

1st) Notice of Receipt for Form I-485, Application To Register Permanent Residence Or Adjust Status

Department of Homeland Security
U.S. Citizenship and Immigration Services

Form I-797C, Notice of Action

THIS NOTICE DOES NOT GRANT ANY IMMIGRATION STATUS OR BENEFIT.

NOTICE TYPE		NOTICE DATE
Receipt		February 11, 2022
CASE TYPE		USCIS ALIEN NUMBER
I-485, Application to Register Permanent Residence or Adjust Status		
RECEIPT NUMBER	RECEIVED DATE	PAGE
[redacted]	February 09, 2022	1 of 1
PRIORITY DATE	PREFERENCE CLASSIFICATION	DATE OF BIRTH
February 09, 2022	Immediate Relative of U.S. citizen	[redacted]

[redacted]
C/O EKATERINA HUFF HUFF LAW PLC
11815 FOUNTAIN WAY STE 300
NEWPORT NEWS, VA 23606

8 00002115

NAME AND MAILING ADDRESS

PAYMENT INFORMATION:

Application/Petition Fee:	$1,140.00
Biometrics Fee:	$85.00
Total Amount Received:	$1,225.00
Total Balance Due:	$0.00

We have received your form and are currently processing the above case. If this notice contains a priority date, this priority does not reflect earlier retained priority dates. We will notify you separately about any other case you filed.

If we determine you must submit biometrics, we will mail you a biometrics appointment notice with the time and place of your appointment.

If you have questions or need to update your personal information listed above, please visit the USCIS Contact Center webpage at uscis.gov/contactcenter to connect with a live USCIS representative in English or Spanish.

USCIS Office Address:
USCIS
National Benefits Center
P.O. Box 648003
Lee's Summit, MO 64002

USCIS Contact Center Number:
(800)375-5283
ATTORNEY COPY
[redacted]

If this is an interview or biometrics appointment notice, please see the back of this notice for important information. Form I-797C 04/01/19

1st) Notice of Receipt for Form I-765, Application For Employment Authorization

Department of Homeland Security
U.S. Citizenship and Immigration Services

Form I-797C, Notice of Action

THIS NOTICE DOES NOT GRANT ANY IMMIGRATION STATUS OR BENEFIT.

NOTICE TYPE		NOTICE DATE
Receipt		February 11, 2022
CASE TYPE		USCIS ALIEN NUMBER
I-765, Application for Employment Authorization		
RECEIPT NUMBER	RECEIVED DATE	PAGE
[redacted]	February 09, 2022	1 of 1
		DATE OF BIRTH [redacted]

[redacted]
C/O EKATERINA HUFF HUFF LAW PLC 8 00002112
11815 FOUNTAIN WAY STE 300
NEWPORT NEWS, VA 23606

NAME AND MAILING ADDRESS

PAYMENT INFORMATION:

Application/Petition Fee:	$0.00
Total Amount Received:	$0.00
Total Balance Due:	$0.00

Eligibility Category: C09

We have received your form and are currently processing the above case. If this notice contains a priority date, this priority does not reflect earlier retained priority dates. We will notify you separately about any other case you filed.

If we determine you must submit biometrics, we will mail you a biometrics appointment notice with the time and place of your appointment.

If you have questions or need to update your personal information listed above, please visit the USCIS Contact Center webpage at uscis.gov/contactcenter to connect with a live USCIS representative in English or Spanish.

This notice, by itself, does not grant any immigration status or benefit, nor is it evidence that this case is still pending. However, this Notice of Action automatically extends the validity of your Employment Authorization Document (EAD) for up to 180 days from the expiration date printed on the front of the card and can be used for employment eligibility verification (Form I-9) purposes if:

- You have timely filed to renew your current Form I-766, Employment Authorization Document (EAD);
- Your EAD renewal is under a category that is eligible for an automatic 180-day extension (see uscis.gov/i-765 for a list of categories);
- The category on your current EAD matches the "Class Requested" listed on this notice (if you are a TPS beneficiary or applicant, your EAD and this notice must contain either the A12 or C19 category, but they do not need to match each other); and
- You do not receive your renewal EAD before your current EAD expires.

If we deny your renewal application, the automatic extension immediately ends and cannot be used for Form I-9 purposes. If your EAD is a combo card, the automatic extension does not apply to advance parole.

If we have approved or are still processing your underlying Form I-140 and your Form I-485 has been pending for at least 180 days, you may request to change employers under INA 204(j). For more information on this process, please visit uscis.gov/i-485supj

USCIS Office Address:
USCIS
National Benefits Center
P.O. Box 648003
Lee's Summit, MO 64002

USCIS Contact Center Number:
(800)375-5283
ATTORNEY COPY
[redacted]

If this is an interview or biometrics appointment notice, please see the back of this notice for important information. Form I-797C 04/01/19

1st) Notice of Receipt for Form I-131, Application For Travel Document

Department of Homeland Security
U.S. Citizenship and Immigration Services

Form I-797C, Notice of Action

THIS NOTICE DOES NOT GRANT ANY IMMIGRATION STATUS OR BENEFIT.

NOTICE TYPE Receipt		NOTICE DATE February 11, 2022
CASE TYPE I-131, Application for Travel Document		USCIS ALIEN NUMBER
RECEIPT NUMBER [redacted]	RECEIVED DATE February 09, 2022	PAGE 1 of 1
		DATE OF BIRTH [redacted]

[redacted]
C/O EKATERINA HUFF HUFF LAW PLC
11815 FOUNTAIN WAY STE 300
NEWPORT NEWS, VA 23606

8 00002113

NAME AND MAILING ADDRESS

PAYMENT INFORMATION:

Application/Petition Fee:	$0.00
Total Amount Received:	$0.00
Total Balance Due:	$0.00

We have received your form and are currently processing the above case. If this notice contains a priority date, this priority does not reflect earlier retained priority dates. We will notify you separately about any other case you filed.

If we determine you must submit biometrics, we will mail you a biometrics appointment notice with the time and place of your appointment.

If you have questions or need to update your personal information listed above, please visit the USCIS Contact Center webpage at uscis.gov/contactcenter to connect with a live USCIS representative in English or Spanish.

USCIS Office Address:
USCIS
National Benefits Center
P.O. Box 648003
Lee's Summit, MO 64002

USCIS Contact Center Number:
(800)375-5283
ATTORNEY COPY
[redacted]

If this is an interview or biometrics appointment notice, please see the back of this notice for important information.

Form I-797C 04/01/19

2nd) Notice of Biometrics Appointment

Department of Homeland Security
U.S. Citizenship and Immigration Services

Form I-797C, Notice of Action

THIS NOTICE DOES NOT GRANT ANY IMMIGRATION STATUS OR BENEFIT.

ASC Appointment Notice	CASE TYPE I485; I765		NOTICE DATE 02/19/2022
APPLICATION/PETITION/REQUEST NUMBER [redacted]		USCIS A# [redacted]	CODE 3
ACCOUNT NUMBER [redacted]	TCR	SERVICE CENTER NBC	PAGE 1 of 2

[redacted]
c/o EKATERINA HUFF
HUFF LAW PLC
11815 FOUNTAIN WAY STE 300
NEWPORT NEWS VA 23606

PLEASE READ THIS ENTIRE NOTICE CAREFULLY. To process your application, petition, or request, U.S. Citizenship and Immigration Services (USCIS) must collect your biometrics. Please appear at the below Application Support Center (ASC) at the date and time specified.

IF YOU FAIL TO APPEAR AS SCHEDULED, YOUR APPOINTMENT MAY NOT BE RESCHEDULED. TO REQUEST THAT USCIS RESCHEDULE YOUR APPOINTMENT, SEE THE INSTRUCTIONS AT THE BOTTOM OF THIS NOTICE. IF USCIS DOES NOT RESCHEDULE YOUR APPOINTMENT, YOUR APPLICATION, PETITION, OR REQUEST WILL BE CONSIDERED ABANDONED AND DENIED.

APPLICATION SUPPORT CENTER	DATE AND TIME OF APPOINTMENT
USCIS NORFOLK 5678 E Virginia Beach Blvd Norfolk VA 23502	03/15/2022 01:00PM

WHEN YOU APPEAR AT THE ASC FOR BIOMETRICS SUBMISSION, YOU MUST BRING:

1. **THIS APPOINTMENT NOTICE.** If you received multiple ASC notices, bring **all** notices to your first appointment, and
2. **PHOTO IDENTIFICATION.** Your biometrics will not be collected without identification. You must bring a valid government-issued photo identification document. If the name on your identification is different than the name on your ASC notice, bring supporting documentation. If you filed an Application for Naturalization (Form N-400) or Application to Replace Permanent Resident Card (Form I-90), you must bring your Permanent Resident Card (also known as a Green Card).

Only those necessary to assist you with transportation or completion of the biometrics worksheet should accompany you to your ASC appointment. If you have open wounds, bandages, or casts when you appear for biometrics submission, USCIS may reschedule your appointment if we determine your injuries may interfere with biometrics submission. Please do not visit a USCIS office if you are sick or feel any symptoms of being sick. Follow the instructions on this notice to reschedule your appointment.

You may bring cell phones or electronic devices, but they must be turned off during biometrics collection. No one may photograph or record at an ASC.

For more information regarding your ASC appointment, visit https://www.uscis.gov/forms/forms-information/preparing-your-biometric-services-appointment. If you have questions regarding this notice, please call the USCIS Contact Center at 1-800-375-5283 (TTY 800-767-1833).

NOTE: If an ASC closes due to inclement weather or unforeseen circumstances, USCIS will automatically reschedule your appointment for the next available date and time. For the latest information on the status of an office, visit https://www.uscis.gov/about-us/uscis-office-closings. Please check this page on the day of your appointment. If USCIS reschedules your appointment for any reason, you will receive a new ASC appointment notice.

To ensure you receive all correspondence from USCIS, you must update your address if you move. For instructions, visit https://www.uscis.gov/addresschange.

USCIS may use your biometrics to check the criminal history records of the FBI, for identity verification, to determine eligibility, to create immigration documents (e.g., Green Card, Employment Authorization Document, etc.), or any purpose authorized by the Immigration and Nationality Act. You may obtain a copy of your own FBI record using the procedures outlined within Title 28 C.F.R., Section 16.32. For information, please visit https://www.fbi.gov/services/cjis/identity-history-summary-checks. For Privacy Act information, please visit https://www.fbi.gov/services/cjis/compact-council/privacy-act-statement.

REQUESTS TO RESCHEDULE/SPECIAL HANDLING

If you are unable to attend your scheduled ASC appointment, you may request that USCIS reschedule your appointment by calling the USCIS Contact Center at 1-800-375-5283 (TTY 800-767-1833). **Your request to reschedule must: 1) be made before the date and time of the original appointment and 2) establish good cause for rescheduling.** If you fail to make a request before your scheduled appointment or fail to establish good cause, USCIS may not reschedule your ASC appointment. If USCIS does not reschedule your appointment, your application, petition, or request will be considered abandoned and denied.

If you have a serious ongoing medical condition and you cannot leave your home/hospital, you may request a mobile biometrics/homebound appointment by following the instructions on the back in the Notice for People with Disabilities or by visiting uscis.gov/accommodations.

APPLICATION NUMBER	APPLICATION NUMBER 2
[redacted]	[redacted]

If you have any questions regarding this notice, please contact the USCIS Contact Center at 1-800-375-5283.

If this is an interview or biometrics appointment notice, please see the back of this notice for important information. Form I-797C 04/01/19

3rd) Notice of Approval for Form I-765, Application For Employment Authorization

Department of Homeland Security
U.S. Citizenship and Immigration Services

Form I-797C, Notice of Action

THIS NOTICE DOES NOT GRANT ANY IMMIGRATION STATUS OR BENEFIT.

Receipt Number	USCIS Account Number	Case Type
MSC[redacted]		I765 - APPLICATION FOR EMPLOYMENT AUTHORIZATION
Received Date 04/30/2021	**Priority Date**	**Applicant** [redacted]
Notice Date 11/30/2021	**Page** 1 of 2	

HUFF LAW PLC
c/o EKATERINA HUFF
11815 FOUNTAIN WAY STE 300
NEWPORT NEWS VA 23606

Notice Type: Approval Notice
Class: C09P
Valid from 11/30/2021 to 11/29/2023

We have mailed an official notice about this case (and any relevant documentation) according to the mailing preferences you chose on Form G-28, Notice of Entry of Appearance as Attorney or Accredited Representative. **This is a courtesy copy, not the official notice.**

What the Official Notice Said

We have approved your application for employment authorization and advance parole based on your pending Form I-485, Application to Register Permanent Residence or Adjust Status. We will send your Employment Authorization Document (also known as an EAD card or Form I-766) to you separately. The EAD card will have an I-512 endorsement on it, which indicates that you have been approved for advance parole.

Your EAD card is proof that you are allowed to work in the United States. Show the card to your employer to verify your authorization to work during the dates on the card. You cannot use this approval notice as proof of your employment authorization.

When you receive your EAD card, please check that all the information on the card is correct. If you need to change any information on the card, please mail all of the following to the office listed below:

- A letter explaining what information needs to be corrected,
- Your EAD card,
- A photocopy of this notice, and
- Evidence to show what the correct information should be. For example, if you need to correct your name, submit a copy of your birth certificate or official name change.

If the I-765 was approved for you as a student requesting Optional Practical Training (OPT): Please note that your EAD and your OPT employment authorization will be automatically terminated if you change educational program levels or transfer to another school. Working in the United States without authorization may result in your removal from the United States or denial of re-entry, and remaining in the United States without maintaining status may result in accruing unlawful presence. Consult your Designated School Official for additional details.

Advanced Parole

The I-512 endorsement on your EAD card is proof that, while your Form I-485 is pending, you may travel abroad without abandoning your Form I-485.

Show your unexpired EAD card with the I-512 endorsement to the ship or airline, and it can let you on board to travel to the United States. As long as your EAD card has not expired, you may use it multiple times to request parole into the United States. U.S. Customs and Border Protection (CBP) can parole you into the U.S. for up to one (1) year.

Before you leave the United States, please note the following information:

- Parole into the United States is not guaranteed. In all cases, a CBP officer must still inspect you at a port of entry to determine whether you are eligible to come into the United States according to the terms of this advance parole. Even though USCIS approved your advance parole, CBP may still refuse to parole you into the United States.
- Parole into the United States is not an "admission" into the U.S. If we deny your Form I-485, you may be subject to removal proceedings for being inadmissible to the U.S.
- Unlawful Presence. If you leave the United States after being unlawfully present in the United States, you may be barred from admission even if you obtained advance parole. If you were unlawfully present in the United States for more than 180 days but less than one year and you leave the U.S. voluntarily before the start of removal proceedings, you are inadmissible for three years; if you were unlawfully present for one year or more, you are inadmissible for ten years.

If you have concerns about how traveling abroad with your EAD card may affect your legal rights, admissibility, or waivers, you should contact an immigration attorney or an immigrant assistance organization accredited by the Board of Immigration Appeals before making foreign travel plans.

Please see the additional information on the back. You will be notified separately about any other cases you filed.

USCIS encourages you to sign up for a USCIS online account. To learn more about creating an account and the benefits, go to https://www.uscis.gov/file-online.

National Benefits Center
U.S. CITIZENSHIP & IMMIGRATION SVC
P.O. Box 648003
Lee's Summit MO 64002

[redacted]

USCIS Contact Center: www.uscis.gov/contactcenter

If this is an interview or biometrics appointment notice, please see the back of this notice for important information. Form I-797C 04/01/19

3rd) Notice of Approval for Form I-131, Application For Travel Document

Department of Homeland Security
U.S. Citizenship and Immigration Services

Form I-797C, Notice of Action

THIS NOTICE DOES NOT GRANT ANY IMMIGRATION STATUS OR BENEFIT.

Receipt Number MSC[redacted]	**USCIS Online Account Number**	**Case Type** I131 - APPLICATION FOR TRAVEL DOCUMENT
Received Date 04/30/2021	**Priority Date**	**Applicant** [redacted]
Notice Date 11/30/2021	**Page** 1 of 1	

HUFF LAW PLC
c/o EKATERINA HUFF
11815 FOUNTAIN WAY STE 300
NEWPORT NEWS VA 23606

Notice Type: Approval Notice
Valid from 11/30/2021 to 11/29/2023

We have mailed an official notice about this case (and any relevant documentation) according to the mailing preferences you chose on Form G-28, Notice of Entry of Appearance as Attorney or Accredited Representative. **This is a courtesy copy, not the official notice.**

What the Official Notice Said

We have approved your application for an Advanced Parole Document. Your travel document will be mailed to you separately and will show the validity of the document and any travel conditions.

How to Use Your Advance Parole Document

You should take your passport and the Advance Parole Document with you when you leave the U.S. You cannot use the Advance Parole Document in place of your passport. When you return to the U.S., present the Advance Parole Document to the U.S. Customs and Border Protection (CBP) officer who inspects you at the port-of-entry.

Before You Leave the United States

Please note the following information:

- Parole into the United States is not guaranteed. In all cases, a CBP officer must still inspect you at a port of entry to determine whether you are eligible to come into the United States according to the terms of this advance parole. Even though USCIS approved your advance parole, CBP may still refuse to parole you into the United States.
- Parole into the United States is not an "admission" into the U.S. If you have a pending Form I-485 and we deny it, you may be subject to removal proceedings for being inadmissible to the U.S.
- Unlawful Presence. If you leave the United States after being unlawfully present in the United States, you may be barred from admission even if you obtained advance parole. If you were unlawfully present in the United States for more than 180 days but less than one year and you leave the U.S. voluntarily before the start of removal proceedings, you are inadmissible for three years; if you were unlawfully present for one year or more, you are inadmissible for ten years.

THIS FORM IS NOT A VISA AND MAY NOT BE USED IN PLACE OF A VISA.

NOTICE: Although this application or petition has been approved, USCIS and the U.S. Department of Homeland Security reserve the right to verify this information before and/or after making a decision on your case so we can ensure that you have complied with applicable laws, rules, regulations, and other legal authorities. We may review public information and records, contact others by mail, the internet or phone, conduct site inspections of businesses and residences, or use other methods of verification. We will use the information obtained to determine whether you are eligible for the benefit you seek. If we find any derogatory information, we will follow the law in determining whether to provide you (and the legal representative listed on your Form G-28, if you submitted one) an opportunity to address that information before we make a formal decision on your case or start proceedings.

Please see the additional information on the back. We will notify you separately about any other cases you have filed.

USCIS encourages you to sign up for a USCIS online account. To learn more about creating an account and the benefits, go to https://www.uscis.gov/file-online.

National Benefits Center
U.S. CITIZENSHIP & IMMIGRATION SVC
P.O. Box 648003
Lee's Summit MO 64002

[redacted]

USCIS Contact Center: www.uscis.gov/contactcenter

If this is an interview or biometrics appointment notice, please see the back of this notice for important information. Form I-797C 04/01/19

4th) Notice of Green Card Interview

Department of Homeland Security
U.S. Citizenship and Immigration Services

Form I-797C, Notice of Action

THIS NOTICE DOES NOT GRANT ANY IMMIGRATION STATUS OR BENEFIT.

REQUEST FOR APPLICANT TO APPEAR FOR INITIAL INTERVIEW			Notice Date March 09, 2022
Case Type FORM I485, APPLICATION TO REGISTER PERMANENT RESIDENCE OR ADJUST STATUS			A# A[redacted]
Receipt Number MSC[redacted]	Received Date April 30, 2021	Priority Date	Page 1 of 2

[redacted]
c/o EKATERINA HUFF
11815 FOUNTAIN WAY STE 300
NEWPORT NEWS VA 23606

A Number
[redacted]
Receipt Number
[redacted]

You are notified to appear before a USCIS officer regarding the application identified above and any supporting applications or petitions at the date, time, and place indicated below. *Failure to appear for the scheduled appointment and/or failure to bring the below listed items will result in the denial of your application.* (8 CFR 103.2 (b)(13))

To ensure visitor and employee health and safety, please pay special attention to the sections entitled, "COVID-19 Safety Precautions" and "Who should come with you?"

YOU MUST APPEAR FOR THIS INTERVIEW - However, if you are ill, have any symptoms of illness, have traveled outside the United States within the past 10 days* (unless you traveled outside of the United States in a personal vehicle) or had contact with a person who tested positive for COVID-19 within the past 14 days; or are at heightened risk due to age or an underlying health condition and would like to reschedule your appointment, call the U.S. Citizenship and Immigration Services (USCIS) Contact Center at 1-800-375-5283 (TTY 1-800-767-1833) as soon as possible to reschedule your appointment. There is no penalty for requesting that your appointment be rescheduled. If you have been fully vaccinated for COVID-19 (defined as at least 2 weeks after second dose of Pfizer and Moderna vaccine, or 2 weeks after single J&J vaccine), you do not need to reschedule after contact with a positive person as long as you continue to not have symptoms.

COVID-19 Safety Precautions - To ensure the health and safety of all who enter USCIS offices, you must take the following safety precautions when arriving for your interview:

- DO NOT arrive more than 15 minutes prior to your interview time. You will not be permitted entry into the office until 15 minutes before your interview.
- If your area has high or substantial COVID-19 transmission rates per the CDC, you and anyone permitted to come with you to your interview (as explained in the section, "Who should come with you?" below) must wear a face covering that covers both the mouth and nose while inside USCIS facilities. Masks with exhaust valves, neck gaiters, or bandanas are not allowed. If you do not have an acceptable face covering, we may offer a replacement or reschedule our appointment.
- Follow local USCIS guidance on social distancing while inside USCIS facilities.
- You may have to answer health screening questions before entering.
- Bring a black or blue ink pen with you to your interview.

Who should come with you? Only the following people may come with you to your interview:

- If your eligibility is based on your marriage, your spouse must come with you to the interview.
- If you do not speak English fluently, you should arrange to have an interpreter available by phone. Do not bring an interpreter to the interview. If you need a Sign Language Interpreter or Certified Deaf Interpreter, call the USCIS Contact Center at 1-800-375-5283 as soon as possible.
- Your attorney or authorized representative may come with you to the interview, or be available via phone.
- If your eligibility is based on a parent/child relationship and you are a minor, your petitioning parent must come with you to the interview.
- If you are a minor under 14 years old, a parent or guardian must come with you to the interview.
- If you have a disability and have an individual who assists you, that individual may come with you.

YOU MUST BRING THE FOLLOWING ITEMS WITH YOU: (Please use as a checklist to prepare for your interview)

- This Interview Notice and your Government issued photo identification.
- If required, a completed Form-I693, Report of Medical Examination and Vaccination Record, and/or vaccination supplement in a sealed envelope (unless already submitted). Please see the Form I-693 Instructions for guidance on whether you need a complete medical examination, an updated vaccine supplement only, or neither.
- If required, a completed Form I-864, Affidavit(s) of Support, with all required evidence (unless already submitted). Please see the Form I-864 Instructions for guidance on whether you need a Form I-864. Required evidence for each of your sponsors includes, but is not limited to, the following:
  - Federal Income Tax returns and W-2's, or certified IRS printouts, for the most recent tax year;
  - Letters from each current employer, verifying current rate of pay and average weekly hours, and pay stubs for the past 2 months;
  - Evidence of your sponsor's and/or co-sponsor's United States Citizenship or Lawful Permanent Resident status.
- All documentation establishing your eligibility for Lawful Permanent Resident status. This includes, but is not limited to, proof of status as an asylee, refugee, or a fiancé(e) nonimmigrant.
- Any immigration-related documentation ever issued to you, including any Form I-766, Employment Authorization Document (EAD); Form I-512, Authorization for Advance Parole; and Form I-571, Refugee Travel Document.
- All travel documents used to enter the United States, including Passports; Form I-512, Authorization for Advance Parole; Form I-571 Refugee Travel Document; and Form I-94, Arrival/Departure Record.
- Your Birth Certificate.
- If your Form I-485 is based on a petition filed by a family member, your petitioner's Birth Certificate and your petitioner's evidence of United States Citizenship or Lawful Permanent Resident Status.

If you have questions, please call the USCIS Contact Center at 1-800-375-5283 (hearing impaired TTY service is 1-800-767-1833)

PLEASE COME TO: U.S. Citizenship and Immigration Services 5678 EAST VIRGINIA BEACH BOULEVARD NORFOLK, VA 23502 1	ON: Friday, April 22, 2022 AT: 01:00PM

If this is an interview or biometrics appointment notice, please see the back of this notice for important information. Form I-797C 04/01/19

5th) Notice of Interview Results

U.S. Department of Homeland Security
U.S. Citizenship and Immigration Services
Norfolk Field Office
5678 East Virginia Beach Blvd
Norfolk, VA 23502

HAND DELIVERED AT INTERVIEW

U.S. Citizenship and Immigration Services

April 22, 2022

[redacted]

Interviewing Officer: [redacted]
Form Type: I-485

NOTICE OF INTERVIEW RESULTS

You have just completed your interview. USCIS is unable to complete your case at this time. Your case is being continued until a final decision can be made. Please see below for further explanation.

REASON FOR CONTINUANCE

☒ Your case is being held for review. At this time, USCIS does not require any further information or documents from you. Should further information or documents be required, you will receive a notice in the mail. We may also schedule you for another interview, you will receive a notice in the mail. Otherwise, a final decision will be mailed once your case is complete.

☐ Your I-485 interview is complete. However, your priority date is not current at this time. Your case will be transferred to the National Benefits Center until your priority date becomes current. Once your priority date becomes current, the NBC will make the final decision on your case.

☐ Your case is being transferred to the USCIS office servicing your new address. Should further information or documents be required, you will receive a notice in the mail. USCIS may also schedule you for another interview, you will receive a notice in the mail. Otherwise, a final decision will be mailed once your case is complete.

For additional information, you can use our many online tools (uscis.gov/tools). If you are not able to find the information you need online, you may reach out to the USCIS Contact Center by visiting uscis.gov/contactcenter. Please allow for no less than 120 days before making a status inquiry on your case. If your case was transferred to the TSC or NBC to wait for your priority date to become current, please allow for no less than 120 days after your priority date becomes current before making a status inquiry on your case.

If you change your address, you must file Form AR-11. Form AR-11 information and filing instructions may be obtained from the USCIS website at www.uscis.gov/addresschange.

Sincerely,

Frank C. Reffel
Field Office Director

cc:

6th) Notice of Approval for Form I-130, Petition For Alien Relative

Department of Homeland Security
U.S. Citizenship and Immigration Services

Form I-797C, Notice of Action

THIS NOTICE DOES NOT GRANT ANY IMMIGRATION STATUS OR BENEFIT.

Receipt Number		Case Type
MSC[redacted]		I130 - PETITION FOR ALIEN RELATIVE
Received Date 02/25/2020	**Priority Date** 02/25/2020	**Petitioner** [redacted]
Notice Date 03/09/2021	**Page** 1 of 1	**Beneficiary** [redacted]

[redacted]
c/o EKATERINA BASHLYKOVA HUFF
HUFF LAW PLC
11815 FOUNTAIN WAY STE 300
NEWPORT NEWS VA 23606

Notice Type: Approval Notice
Section: Husband or wife of U.S. Citizen, 201(b) INA

We have mailed an official notice about this case (and any relevant documentation) according to the mailing preferences you chose on Form G-28, Notice of Entry of Appearance as Attorney or Accredited Representative. **This is a courtesy copy, not the official notice.**

What the Official Notice Said

The above petition has been approved. The beneficiary of this petition will be notified separately when a decision is reached on his or her pending adjustment of status application.
THIS FORM IS NOT A VISA AND MAY NOT BE USED IN PLACE OF A VISA.

The approval of this visa petition does not in itself grant any immigration status and does not guarantee that the alien beneficiary will subsequently be found to be eligible for a visa, for admission to the United States, or for an extension, change, or adjustment of status.
NOTICE: Although this application or petition has been approved, USCIS and the U.S. Department of Homeland Security reserve the right to verify this information before and/or after making a decision on your case so we can ensure that you have complied with applicable laws, rules, regulations, and other legal authorities. We may review public information and records, contact others by mail, the internet or phone, conduct site inspections of businesses and residences, or use other methods of verification. We will use the information obtained to determine whether you are eligible for the benefit you seek. If we find any derogatory information, we will follow the law in determining whether to provide you (and the legal representative listed on your Form G-28, if you submitted one) an opportunity to address that information before we make a formal decision on your case or start proceedings.

Please see the additional information on the back. You will be notified separately about any other cases you filed.

National Benefits Center
U. S. CITIZENSHIP & IMMIGRATION SVC
P.O. Box 648003
Lee's Summit MO 64002
USCIS Contact Center: www.uscis.gov/contactcenter

[redacted]

If this is an interview or biometrics appointment notice, please see the back of this notice for important information. Form I-797C 04/01/19

6th) Notice of Approval for Form I-485, Application To Register Permanent Residence Or Adjust Status

Department of Homeland Security
U.S. Citizenship and Immigration Services

Form I-797C, Notice of Action

THIS NOTICE DOES NOT GRANT ANY IMMIGRATION STATUS OR BENEFIT.

Receipt Number		Case Type
MSC[redacted]		I485 - APPLICATION TO REGISTER PERMANENT RESIDENCE OR ADJUST STATUS
Received Date 02/25/2020	Priority Date 02/25/2020	Applicant [redacted]
Notice Date 03/09/2021	Page 1 of 1	Beneficiary [redacted]

[redacted]
c/o EKATERINA BASHLYKOVA HUFF
HUFF LAW PLC
11815 FOUNTAIN WAY STE 300
NEWPORT NEWS VA 23606

Notice Type: Approval Notice
Section: Immediate Relative of U.S. citizen
COA: CR6

We have mailed an official notice about this case (and any relevant documentation) according to the mailing preferences you chose on Form G-28, Notice of Entry of Appearance as Attorney or Accredited Representative. **This is a courtesy copy, not the official notice.**

What the Official Notice Said

WELCOME TO THE UNITED STATES OF AMERICA

This is to notify you that your application for permanent residence has been approved. It is with great pleasure that we welcome you to permanent resident status in the United States.

At the top of this notice you will see a very important number. It is your USCIS A# (A-Number). This is your permanent resident account and file number. This permanent account number is very important to you. You will need it whenever you contact us.

We will soon mail you a new *Permanent Resident Card.* You should receive it within the next 3 weeks. You can use it to show your new status. When you receive your card you must carry it with you at all times if you are 18 or older. It is the law.

Please call us at **(800) 375-5283** if any of the information about you shown above is incorrect, if you move before you receive your card, or if you don't receive your card within the next 3 weeks. If you call us, please have your A# and also the receipt number shown above available. The receipt number is a tracking number for your application.

Please read the notice that comes with your card. It will have important information about your card, about your status and responsibilities, and about permanent resident services available to you.

Your new card will expire two years from when you became a permanent resident. By law your resident status is conditional and you must apply to remove those conditions before your card expires. We recommend you apply several months before your card expires. When the time comes and you need filing information, or an application, or if you ever have other questions about permanent resident services available to you, just call our *National Customer Service Center* at **1-800-375-5283** or visit the USCIS website at **www.uscis.gov**. (If you are hearing impaired, the NCSC's TDD number is **1-800-767-1833**.) The best days to call the NCSC are Tuesday through Friday.

Once again, welcome to the United States and congratulations on your permanent resident status.
THIS FORM IS NOT A VISA AND MAY NOT BE USED IN PLACE OF A VISA.

NOTICE: Although this application or petition has been approved, USCIS and the U.S. Department of Homeland Security reserve the right to verify this information before and/or after making a decision on your case so we can ensure that you have complied with applicable laws, rules, regulations, and other legal authorities. We may review public information and records, contact others by mail, the internet or phone, conduct site inspections of businesses and residences, or use other methods of verification. We will use the information obtained to determine whether you are eligible for the benefit you seek. If we find any derogatory information, we will follow the law in determining whether to provide you (and the legal representative listed on your Form G-28, if you submitted one) an opportunity to address that information before we make a formal decision on your case or start proceedings.

Please see the additional information on the back. You will be notified separately about any other cases you filed.

National Benefits Center
U. S. CITIZENSHIP & IMMIGRATION SVC
P.O. Box 648003
Lee's Summit MO 64002
USCIS Contact Center: www.uscis.gov/contactcenter

[redacted]

If this is an interview or biometrics appointment notice, please see the back of this notice for important information. Form I-797C 04/01/19

Last) Actual Green Card

NOTES

Made in the USA
Monee, IL
05 November 2026

67386570R00059